Intercultural dialogue

Mary Louise Pratt, Ron G. Manley, Susan Bassnett

With an introduction by
Nick Wadham-Smith

Series
Ros

First published 2004
British Council
10 Spring Gardens
London SW1A 2BN
www.britishcouncil.org

ISBN 0-86355-537-3

Cover design by Atelier Works

Contents

Preface

by the Director-General

The British Council seeks to build long-term relationships between people of different cultures. Our currency is trust. The British Council has been a leader in cultural relations since its founding in 1934. In order to celebrate our 70th anniversary, I asked Counterpoint, our think tank on cultural relations, to commission a series of ten sets of essays, each set looking at a central issue from a variety of angles and viewpoints. The issues range from European enlargement to 'Britishness', and from the significance of death to the role of faith and the nature of secularism.

The 34 writers come from all over the world, though at least one in each set is British. Each introduction, with one exception, is written by a member of British Council staff. They testify to the richness of the intellectual and moral resource that the British Council represents.

Our intention is to stimulate debate rather than arrive at consensus. Some essays are controversial. None of them expresses, individually, a British Council viewpoint. They are the work of individual authors of distinction from whom we have sought views. But collectively, they represent something more than the sum of their parts – a commitment to the belief that dialogue is the essential heart of cultural relations.

Dialogue requires and generates trust. The biggest danger in what is often called public diplomacy work is that we simply broadcast views, policies, values and positions. A senior European diplomat recently said at a British Council conference: 'The world is fed up with hearing us talk. What it wants is for us to shut up and listen.' Listening and demonstrating our commitment to the free and creative interplay of ideas is an indispensable pre-condition for building trust.

To build trust we must engage in effective, open dialogue. Increased mutual understanding based on trust, whether we agree or disagree, is a precious outcome.

David Green KCMG

Introduction

Nick Wadham-Smith

Among weapons of mass destruction, chemical weapons occupy a special place: specifically they target people, leaving the physical infrastructure of their societies mainly intact. Their victims, who are killed in large numbers, are lucky if they die quickly. Buildings, railways, hospitals and homes remain standing to be resettled or left empty. These weapons are profoundly anti-human: the weapon of choice for those who would destroy cultures when they fail to understand them.

The essays in this volume by two distinguished thinkers about language and communication across cultures, Susan Bassnett and Mary Louise Pratt, set out to trace the outlines of a new humanism by drawing on the potential of a gradually emerging global order. Given their reflections on the planetary dimension of what it is to be human, it is doubly appropriate that Ron Manley joins them to tell us how the Organisation for the Prohibition of Chemical Weapons (OPCW) was set up. A fascinating story of how a multinational secretariat and inspectorate were recruited and unified into a force to monitor and control those most inhuman of weapons, it both illuminates and is illuminated by the writings of his two companions.

The building of OPCW was so unusual from an organisational point of view because it required the bringing together of a large team of 68 nationalities for a single professional purpose. This is where intercultural specialists start to get interested. Most conventional studies of communication problems deal with relatively accidental interactions of cultures – as when the headquarters staff of a multinational company encounter its local employees and customers in an 'overseas' context. Business generates the initial challenge and determines the appropriate solution. With OPCW, it was a deliberate cultural strategy to bring a multinational mix of 220 inspectors and 500 technical personnel together in The Hague:

> 'The key to the creation of a successful international organisation was to recruit staff with the ability to work and function well in a multinational and multicultural environment.'

Manley relates how candidates were found and selected, observing in passing how the application form was interpreted and completed in different cultures. We glimpse individuals, plucked from their positions within existing hierarchies, operating in the altogether flatter terrain of the new context. Vital training needs arose: the analytical chemists, for example, 'were provided with extensive training in the collection and analysis of samples in the field and the procedures necessary to ensure their integrity and accurate analysis' – (how many dramatic dilemmas lie behind this calm description!). Member states saw to the policy but it was up to the Secretariat to put it into practice and solve the ensuing problems. Twelve nationalities around a table would produce at least 13 solutions. Consensus was reached by metaphorically locking everyone in until they agreed. As well as the different cultures of the nations involved, there were different parts of the organisational culture, the Secretariat vs the Inspectorate, to contend with.

Perhaps it is the issue of language that provides the strongest link with the other arguments in this volume about globalisation. English was the lingua franca of the organisation, but the huge bank of primary languages spoken became an essential resource for translation and cultural interpretation: a speaker of Russian was also an instant guide for his colleagues to the cultures of Russia. English may be in a dominant global position but those who use it are not necessarily the target of a neo-imperialist marketing campaign for the cultures of Britain, the USA and Australasia. As Susan Bassnett points out, second language speakers are especially privileged:

> 'Those who have learned English in addition to their own language or languages are able to acquire an understanding of the difficulties of communicating across cultures that is not possible for monolingual speakers.'

English may be a lingua franca but, as the foreign language educationalist Michael Byram has often observed, it does not have a cultura franca. English has many centres: in addition to 'British' English, dictionaries of other Englishes now fill the shelf: Australian, Canadian, Caribbean, Hiberno-, Indian, Jamaican, Liberian, Malaysian, New Zealand, Philippine, Scottish, Singapore and South African. English is now spoken more by second language users than by first, its obliging malleability at the service of communicators both within and between cultures.

In all discussions about intercultural communication, issues of universalism loom large: this is so for both Pratt and Bassnett. Bassnett sees language learning as fundamental to a critique of universalist reductionism:

> 'Knowledge of more than one language soon exposes the fallacy of universal claims. Of course the human body suffers pain, hunger, joy and grief everywhere in the world, but how those emotions manifest themselves, how they are internalised and then narrated is not universal . . . simply assuming that we are communicating perfectly because other people speak a version of English is dangerous, because it is premised on an assumption of sameness between cultures that is patently false. Knowledge of different languages is a first step, because then we can begin to grasp the immense differences between cultures, and start to explore ways of building bridges.'

And for Mary Louise Pratt, 'it is impossible to think seriously about intercultural dialogue without coming to grips with the linguistic dimensions of today's planetary social, ecological, economic, political and imaginary realignments'. Language not only mediates these changes but also the way in which we think about them.

For Pratt, the 'rapidly accelerating movement of peoples is creating not a world without history, but the proliferating intersection of histories'. Taking two fascinating examples of intercultural dialogue, one from a classroom in eastern Europe, the other from a street corner in Manhattan, she unpicks the complexities of intercultural exchange and expands her celebrated concept of the 'Contact Zone' between cultures ('social spaces where cultures meet, clash, and grapple with each other, often in contexts of highly asymmetrical relations of power, such as colonialism, slavery, or their aftermaths'). Her analysis culminates in a very impressive move to rehabilitate humanism in the service of a new 'planetary' political order. This involves restoring a universal dimension to humanism, which avoids charges of being merely 'occidental', and which can be confident in the face of difference. We might characterise this in philosophical terms as an attempt to replace an *essential* humanism, one which pre-exists as a conceptual system in the mind, by showing how it actually depends on a *contingent* universalism – in this case, a global critical mass of similar beliefs about what constitutes humanity. She urges us to oppose 'the doctrine many Westerners have installed in their heads: the human was invented by humanism'.

In order to show how it connects with Susan Bassnett's main themes and resonates very powerfully for all those working in cultural relations, let me single out one argument with which Pratt meets the multicultural objections to a universal humanism.

Many object to the project of humanism because it excludes certain identity groups who are considered on a liberal calculus to be oppositional on some scale, moving from, say, 'indigenous peoples' on one side to 'insurgent' through 'freedom fighter' to 'terrorist'. Pratt argues that identity groups, 'take form as such after long and persistent efforts to achieve inclusion and access, especially to the political process, have taken place and have not succeeded'. It is the failure to address or even acknowledge this fact that freezes a cultural identity into the category of the non-negotiable. The act of recognition is missing and, closely allied to it, the offer of apology.

Bassnett focuses on the performance of apology. She takes an example of a politician, President George W. Bush Jr, who offers an apology for the treatment of Iraqi prisoners-of-war. However, because the apology is in the form of a personal confession – 'I am sorry' – it focuses on the speaker and does not address those in a different cultural frame of reference, who need to be given the opportunity to forgive.

Working in the British Council's cultural relations think tank, I am just as interested in why cultural relations can fail as in how they can succeed. This example of apology shows two major reasons why dialogue can founder. If we do not understand how communication is taking place, the ways in which an encounter between different cultures is structured, we are at a huge disadvantage. Knowledge is involved, of the linguistic and extra-linguistic factors. But self-awareness is equally important since it enables us to glimpse the hidden dimensions of power and difference at work in communication and enter a virtuous circle: the more we engage in dialogue, the more we learn about ourselves and the more we show our capacity to reflect and change, the more we engender trust and reflection in others. This awareness is also of the historical self, the past of the national and other communities we belong to. For example, in talking of chemical weapons, it should be part of my knowledge, that in the 1920s, the British Royal Air Force used poisoned gas to 'control' those Arabs and Kurds in Iraq who stood in the way of the imperial plan.

If we think that entering the virtuous circle of intercultural dialogue is a matter of choice for those, like me, who work in cultural relations, then the authors of this volume say we are wrong: it is an imperative. Much intercultural dialogue happens without the intervention of organisations such as the British Council and, as Mary Louise Pratt observes: 'Conflict is not an inevitable by-product of cultural difference.' However she correctly points out that 'differences can always erupt into conflict, or be manipulated into conflict.' It is that manufactured species of conflict which it is the duty of cultural relations to deconstruct. That challenge will be met only by a fiercely independent courage to draw on the widest consensus of humanity and the deepest understanding of ourselves and others.

Planetarity *

Mary Louise Pratt

I

In December 2002 the following e-mail message appeared on my screen, from a young Canadian teaching English composition in Blagoevgrad, Bulgaria. The reference is to an essay I wrote in 1991 called *Arts of the Contact Zone*, that was widely reprinted in American college textbooks. It offered a template for thinking about multiculturalism, multicultural pedagogy and democracy in the Americas:[1]

Dear Dr Pratt

I just thought you might like to know: I assigned your 'Contact Zone' piece from Ways of Reading *to students here at the American University in Bulgaria. AUBG was established here after the fall of communism with the aim of teaching critical thinking and leadership on the model of an American liberal arts college. About 75 per cent of the students are Bulgarian, and the rest come, mostly, on scholarship from countries ranging from Croatia to Mongolia. In a first-year composition course I asked students to write an essay making suggestions for a course on Balkan civilisation. I got a wide range of responses.*

1 *Most students stressed the study of history, suggesting that students compare school textbook accounts of single events in the history of the region, and work carefully toward consensus*

---

* Planetarity: Gayatri Chakravorty Spivak uses this term as a category of analysis in her recent book *Death of a Discipline*, New York, Columbia University Press, 2003.

on what actually happened. Not one student thinks this consensus would actually be achieved, but most think it would be worthwhile to push the discussion as far as can be done. One student suggested the perhaps dangerous technique of showing a highly nationalist anti-Turkish Bulgarian historical film as a centre for discussion.

2 *One student suggested interviews with students of other nationalities to find out what ethnic jokes are being told about one's own ethnicity.*

3 *One student suggested that the issue of religion should be approached through its place in daily life rather than through theology or general principles, saying people would find it easier to sympathise across confessional lines that way.*

4 *Serbian students without exception blasted their previous education as corrupted by nationalism. The war has had a deep effect on them, and the quandary of being a Serb in 2002 is a significant concern for them. Kosovar Albanians, in contrast, are not especially preoccupied with the issues of the war.*

5 *Several students thought the study of linguistics would help a class like this. Some Bulgarian students thought that it might be scientifically proven that Macedonian is really a kind of Bulgarian. Other students thought that the incontrovertible presence of foreign, especially Turkish, words in each language, would help to dismantle myths of national purity.*

6 *Students stressed the demands on the professor in a class like this, saying that principles would be less important than social skills in context. All who mentioned the issue expressed a preference for an outsider rather than a person of Balkan nationality.*

7 *A few Bulgarian students devoted parts of their essays to reaffirming their belief in nationalist Bulgarian views of Balkan history: '500 years of the Ottoman yoke', etc.*

8 *Some students came to realise that they knew more about France than about the country next door.*

9 *A cohesive group took issue with you on the issue of nation, saying the idea of 'imagined community' doesn't do justice to nation as they experience it.*

So, your paper at the MLA years ago is still echoing here in Blagoevgrad.
Sincerely
Matthew de Coursey

No one is more suspicious than I am of exported imperial education models. Nevertheless I found the message moving. Here was a teacher putting a piece of writing to work across time, distance, and difference to enable reflection on an unprecedented and traumatised present, on the pasts that made it, on possible futures, and on learning itself. Mr de Coursey's classroom was a self-conscious exercise in intercultural dialogue. The nine points the class passed on had the makings of a book of wisdom on how to conduct such dialogues.

Point one specifies the importance of rewriting history. Equally important, it describes the exercise of creating provisional communities across lines of difference through a pursuit of consensus. The pursuit need not actually produce consensus in order to succeed in enacting a provisional community and mediating differences.

Point two specifies the power of converting difference into reciprocity, that is, of enacting or performing difference as reciprocity. This is a form of cultural agency.[2]

Point three calls for privileging the lived experience of differences over the knowledge, beliefs, and ideologies that codify them. At the level of belief, differences readily translate into incompatibilities – 'clashes of civilisations.' But difference is lived as coexistence, the co-presence of bodies in spaces – the uneasy arts of the Contact Zone.[3]

Points four and five indict essentialism ('myths of national purity') and the instruments that produce it, and identify language as a source of counter-knowledge. Point seven, however, shows how difficult this can be when subaltern hierarchies of power are involved. The Bulgarians reasserted a subaltern identity linked to claims for redress. Once articulated, essentialisms anchored in claims to superiority or redress do not simply go away. They have to be worked through.

Point six highlights the position of the mediator. In this case the role is held by a subject I like to call the 'Committed Outsider', a position many scholars try to occupy as they study and teach literatures, languages and cultures not of their own time or place. In Mr de Coursey's classroom, his displacement and distance, combined with his serious commitment to being where he is, enable him to create the space for the intercultural dialogue. Both the displacement and the commitment are necessary. On the other hand, Mr de Coursey's outsider status is useful only insofar as he is able to recognise and interact with the insider knowledge and experience of those whose dialogue he is sponsoring. The fact that the search for understanding was going on in a lingua franca that was nobody's national tongue was probably quite valuable.

Point eight identifies the role of sanctioned ignorance in producing marginality, and point nine shows the need for marginal subjects to revise and critique concepts (like 'imagined community') in order to refute marginality.

De Coursey's account registers two features that usually characterise intercultural dialogues: performativity and improvisation. By performativity I mean that the 'interculturality' does not consist solely, or even principally, in the content of the dialogue or the meanings produced, but in the fact of its taking place, in the embodied event or practice.[4] Improvisation refers to the obvious fact that what makes intercultural dialogues necessary is a history of their absence; the fact that relations of mutuality and reciprocity have not been present, have broken down, or been detonated into violence. Such relations cannot be conjured out of nowhere or prescribed according to fixed models. They have to be made up out of what is there in the embodied moment. Hence, performativity and improvisation. And these two terms imply a third: imperfection.

Mr De Coursey was seeking to remedy the thing for which his location has provided the master metaphor: balkanisation. Remarkably, he chose a head-on approach: reclaiming that very term by having students imagine a course on Balkan civilisation. He proposed an imagined object whose contours were to be debated through a collective pursuit of truth and understanding in which all the participants are seen as having a stake. It was a risky choice, perhaps, for it engaged the group in the 'civilisational thinking' that so readily produces today's essentialisms. In that light, it's significant that the imagined object was a course on Balkan civilisation, and not Balkan civilisation itself.

Intercultural dialogues often hinge on such inclusive, imagined objects of inquiry. State-sponsored truth commissions are a recent example. In the aftermath of internal wars, such commissions set up high-profile public dialogues that seek to reconcile antagonists around a shared account of events, and thus reconstitute the *polis*. Such commissions assume that the state which went to war on its citizens suppressed the facts about its violence. If the state is again to be legitimate, these facts must be made public and condemned with perpetrators and victims in the same room. Discussion of truth commissions often focuses on their limits and imperfections. But it's helpful to think of 'truth' here not as that which must be fully specified, but (like De Coursey's course on Balkan civilisation) as an imagined object in which the ex-antagonists all have a stake and whose construction is the occasion for their shared agency. Truth commissions, held as public events and often televised, are dramatic examples of the combined force of meaning and performance.
In terms of restoring citizenship, the public performance of truth and the embodied engagement of perpetrators and victims are as important as the facts revealed.

Let me apply the terms I've been using to a second instance of intercultural dialogue from the streets of New York City.

Not long ago I was standing at an intersection in Manhattan beside one of the ubiquitous corner markets that are a New York trademark. A woman's voice, with the Korean accent of the store manager, cried 'Water!' and the store's Mexican employee bounded into the street in pursuit of a man who had just stolen a bottle of water. Two delivery workers, a Jamaican and a Guatemalan, stood beside me on the corner. The Jamaican grabbed the Mexican by the arm and gently said, 'No, mon, don't be a fool. You could get yourself killed. Let him go.' A dialogue ensued that ran something like this (with gestures, accents, the performative bleached out by writing):

> Mexicano: But he stole water. It's my job.
> Jamaican: No, it's your job to chase him inside the store, but in the street, let him go. Don't risk your life for 50 cents.
> Mexicano: If I don't stop him, the next guy will come along and do the same thing.
> Jamaican: That's not your problem, mon. It's 50 cents. And not even your 50 cents
> Mexicano: It's not the money. It's the act.
> Jamaican: You have to watch out for yourself. Nobody else cares about you. You don't understand the system.
> Mexicano: No, *you* don't understand the system.

The Guatemalan did not speak enough English to participate. The Committed Outsider (me) offered to translate into Spanish for him, but he seemed to understand well enough, and listened intently. I stood by thinking, 'exchanges like these are producing the future of this city'. Every minute of every day New York's global citizenry is at work exploring and explaining differences, negotiating identities, values, spaces, manners, ethics, tastes, meanings, and the assumptions of mutual responsibility that make collective life work, or fail. Some of this goes on in institutionalised, staged settings like De Coursey's classroom, but most of it takes place informally, embedded in the active course of daily life. Unlike English, romance languages can distinguish between (to use the Spanish terms) *multiculturalismo*, a programmed intervention, and *multiculturalidad*, the given fact of culturally diverse social formations. Whatever happens to the former, the latter is here to stay in most of the world's cities, shaped among other things by the structured inequalities of local and global orders.

In his classroom, De Coursey occasioned the intercultural dialogue by positing an inclusive imaginary object ('Balkan civilisation') around which he asked his students to explore their differences. On the New York street corner, the dialogue arrived at such another object, 'the system'. The speakers came to agreement about the fact that they had different understandings of 'the system'. Each recognised the other's version, and the importance of knowing the system. Difference translated into reciprocity. Provisional community was created across lines of difference through a pursuit of truth that did not need to produce consensus in order to succeed. Again the exchange was improvised, created out of what was in play in the situation where it took place, and it was imperfect (the Guatemalan, for instance, could not participate fully).

Here too performativity was at least as important as the production of meaning. At the level of meaning the Jamaican argued for self-interest and self-preservation. Yet at the level of embodied practice, he was undertaking an act of altruism and solidarity underscored by the gentleness of his words. By his own argument, the safety of the Mexicano was not his problem, yet in making the argument he went out of his way to make it his problem. At the level of argument the Mexicano disagreed with the Jamaican, but at the level of embodied practice, by stopping to talk, he *de facto* took the advice. (The thief defiantly sauntered off.) The dialogue, in other words, went on simultaneously and differently as meaning and performance.

There are old contact zones and new ones. The Balkans have been 'balkanised' as long as anyone can remember – that's why they gave us the metaphor. De Coursey's classroom exemplifies the intercultural work that seeks to refashion long-standing historical relations among well-defined groups whose identities constitute each other. Multiculturalism is perhaps originally associated with this work. Yet multiculturalism as a social and intellectual project was catalysed in the 1970s and 80s by dramatic increases in the global movement of peoples, notably from Africa, Asia and Latin America to North America and Europe.

The New York street corner encounter is a product of these more recent developments. Neo-liberalism had much to do with creating the structures of opportunity and cruel necessity that brought the Korean, the Jamaican, the Mexican, the Guatemalan, and me, to that spot, to our forms of employment, and our places in hierarchies of exploitation. Yet history was profoundly in play there too. The two men's contrasting views of citizenship and responsibility are not idiosyncratic, after all. Behind the Jamaican's arguments is the fractured history of plantation slavery and resistance culture in the Caribbean. Behind the Mexicano's arguments are Mesoamerica's indigenous and agrarian traditions, where prestige is acquired in the community through the acceptance of responsibilities, and rights are contingent on contributing. (In this sense, two differing 'systems' are indeed present here.) Rapidly accelerating movement of peoples is creating not a world without history, but the proliferating intersection of histories.

II

I would like to pick up this question of intersecting histories to approach some recent scholarly arguments about how struggles for justice and well-being should be carried out in a world in which diverse values and competing claims increasingly interact. Intellectuals for a long time now have been bumping up against the limits of Western secular humanism. One of the most conspicuous and consequential of those limits has been the contradiction between universalism and egalitarianism on the one hand, and on the other, the structures of exclusion and otherness without which modernity cannot perceive itself.

The much-maligned identity movements that so disconcerted left and right in the 1980s, based on ethnicity, race, gender and sexuality, rose out of those modernist exclusions. So did many of our current demands for intercultural dialogue. It is interesting to think of those movements in terms of what systems theorists call autopoeisis, 'the generative process whereby everything that lives realises its mode of being'.[5] They converted exclusion and inequality into motors of autopoeisis, producing knowledges, desires, meanings, and agents – intellectuals, artists, critics and politicians. These knowledges were, and still are, heresies seeking to become orthodoxies. A paradigmatic case, and protagonist, has been transnational feminism, a work still in progress. A more recent case is the new worldwide protagonism of indigenous peoples, another work in progress, that began in the 1990s.

From other spaces of intellectuality, however, such autopoeisis from exclusion is continuously denounced as parochial, balkanising, egotistical – a failure of solidarity. The recognition of diversity, some claim, has led to a paralysing relativism that has made it impossible to establish norms to underwrite collective actions and prescriptions across lines of difference. Among conservatives, relativism is seen as a threat to 'God-given' norms about such matters as gender roles, sexual behaviour, hierarchy and authority. At this moment of writing (summer 2004), nationalism, patriotism, and militarism are on the rise in many places, notably Europe and the United States, and religious fundamentalisms have become privileged tools for conducting geopolitical conflict and asserting authoritarianism. Such attempts at forced homogenisation at times look like panicked responses to the complexity of the world, and at others like calculating positionings in what is seen as a competitive global endgame.

On the left, which is the side I'm interested in here, relativism is criticised for making it impossible to legitimate egalitarian values of justice, democracy and rights even though these are deemed 'universal.' The democratic, inclusive impulses of multiculturalism, we hear, leave the left with no authority to prescribe democratic and egalitarian values against authoritarianism and hierarchy on the right.[6] The only way to move forward, say these voices, is to agree to leave behind the wounds of the past that divide us, and meet together again beneath the sign of the European Enlightenment.

In a recent essay called 'Finding our way back to the Enlightenment', for example, New York intellectual Thomas de Zengotita eloquently elaborates the argument. Speaking in the context of the rise of the right in the United States and abroad, de Zengotita argues urgently that Enlightenment humanism is 'the only basis for a coherent ideology capable of uniting progressive forces in this critical hour'.[7] The basis for democratic politics must be:

> 'An identification with humanity in its totality and with each human being . . . in its secular form this identification is rooted in the ideals of Enlightened humanism, ideals articulated by Locke, Rousseau and Kant and put in play historically by the *Bill of Rights* and the *Declaration of the Rights of Man*. However miserably partisans of these principles failed to fulfil them in practice, the principles themselves are unambiguous, and they all depend on that fundamental identification of each of us with all of us, with the sheer human being abstracted in the ideal from concrete contexts of history and tradition.'

We must be open, he insists, to the possibility that 'the modern western tradition has a genuine claim – a superior claim – on the allegiance of humanity after all'. His final advice is that his readers put down Foucault and pick up Voltaire.

I cite Zengotita as representative of an eloquent and vociferous current in contemporary debate about values, defined by its call for a renewed consensus around Enlightenment universalism and rejection of that unloved and elusive villain, identity politics. As attractive and convincing as this position may be, the response of historically excluded groups can be predicted. For the few who have attained a voice in the debate, the idea of what Fred Moten has called a 'voluntary de-racialisation' of the democratic project,[8] or an invitation to voluntarily reneutralise gender, is unacceptable. It would lead directly to the loss of the few spaces excluded groups have tenuously won, and of the social understandings they have brought.

How to exit this impasse? My own argument so far would invite me to see 'the Enlightenment' as an imagined object around which de Zengotita seeks to form a provisional community engaged in a shared pursuit of truth and understanding. The point would be not to arrive at a consensus about the Enlightenment, but to engage in a consensus-building debate. My contribution, however, will be to argue that we need a different imagined object – one that might be called 'the global or planetary human'.

III

It seems to me that this call for a return to the Enlightenment, which has intensified in the USA in the face of rising authoritarianism, is shaped by a pair of misunderstandings that can perhaps be clarified.

The first has to do with the historicity of that snark: identity politics. The so-called identity groups accused of fragmenting the struggle for the common good do not, we know, come from nowhere. They are constituted through lack of access to that common good. This much is agreed on. These exclusions are often understood as ills from the past, to be atoned for or gotten over, or both. Yet (and here is the point often overlooked) the ills of the past acquire significance only because the exclusions are still going on in the present. Identity politics, I would argue, take form as such after groups have made long and persistent efforts to achieve inclusion and access, especially to the political process, and have not succeeded. Only then, I would argue, do identity formations politicise themselves. In the United States, the refusal of the Democratic Party to racially integrate party caucuses in 1962 forced the politicisation of the Black movement. The Zapatista movement in Mexico appeared only after many decades of unsuccessful struggle for recognition and redress by indigenous groups; only after other avenues seemed exhausted. Continued exclusion in the present, not past resentment, explains subordinated groups;' rejection of the homogenising proposal and superior claims of a renewed Enlightenment.

The second misunderstanding has to do with what I have come to call the 'monopolism' of Enlightenment thought.[9] Let me explain. The call for a return to Enlightenment principles as the only alternative for humankind seems to depend to a significant degree on ethnographic and historical error. The error lies in attributing to the Enlightenment a monopoly on those principles, as if nothing like them has ever existed anywhere else in human geography or history. But do we really think that no other cultures have the ability to conceive of humankind as a totality? That the powers of rationality were discovered only once, and in France? Or that, though slavery has existed (and exists) in many places, the idea of freedom has been born only once? That the city is an invention of modernity or of Europe? That cosmopolitanism has been unique to the West?

Take for example the idea of the common good. Historically and ethnographically we know that the idea of the common good is not a unique invention of the European Enlightenment. It has been invented and reinvented since time immemorial. It's been a common good of human groups all over the planet. Not necessarily all human groups but lots of them – there's no need to posit universals here, only multiple genealogies. The claim is just that the idea of the common good has more than one narrative of origin.

Just as the West has never had a monopoly on greed, genocide, enslavement, exploitation, authoritarianism, heterosexism, religious violence, patriarchy and injustice, so the West has not had a monopoly on empiricism, rationality, principles of equality, liberty, justice, the rule of law, the responsibility of the strong toward the weak and the entitlement of all to security and well-being. Elements like these, and indeed the ability, as de Zengotita puts it, to 'identify with humanity in its totality', have had a plural existence throughout the panorama of human societies. (Note again, though, that I am not speaking of universals. My approach doesn't require me to.) De Zengotita fleetingly acknowledges this alternative. Reiterating the modern Western tradition's, 'genuine claims on the allegiance of humanity', he allows a tiny parenthesis: '(there may be other sources for these principles)'. But the point stays right there caged between the parentheses. Common sense in these debates still assumes Enlightenment principles to be the exclusive property of the Enlightenment. In fact that seems to be one of the conventions of the debate, even among critics of what Judith Butler calls the 'colonial, expansionist logic' of Enlightenment universalism.[10]

The argument I'm making has been continuously repeated by post-colonial and progressive multicultural thinkers. Nobel prize-winning economist Amartya Sen, for instance, recently lamented the 'confusion' caused by 'the belief that democracy is a quintessentially Western idea'.[11] This commonplace view, Sen notes, elides the deep diffusion of ancient Greece into the Middle East, India, and Northern Africa, which predates its influence in Europe. More important today, Sen argues, is the 'historical point that while public reasoning flourished in many ways in ancient Greece, it did that also in several other ancient civilizations – sometimes spectacularly so'. He cites examples from India, Japan, and southern Africa, concluding that 'public reasoning in various forms has had a long history across the world, and these traditions in diverse cultures make it hard to see democracy as an essentially Western idea'.

Once you think past the idea of a Western monopoly on what the West denotes as Enlightenment principles, a straightforward alternative appears. It is to dissolve the narrative of the Enlightenment into a planetary human history whose elements – not necessarily universals – have been invented and reinvented in more times and places than we will ever know. What de Zengotita calls the ideals of Enlightenment humanism, including the idea of 'humanity in its totality and each human being' need not be subsumed into the epic of occident, with its vast imperial contradictions. Rather, what appears is what Caribbean scholar Sylvia Wynter calls 'a new semantic charter', a '*humanitas* now conceived as isomorphic with the global human rather than with merely its Indo-European expression'.[12]

The global human may sound like an idealist proposal, or a naïve reaffirmation of innate human goodness, or an inversion of the civilisation–barbarism polarity, or a rehomogenisation of the species. But it is none of these. Above all it is not a universalist proposal. Rather it tries to solve the problems universalism raises.

When one lets go of the commonsense idea of the metropolitan monopoly on Enlightenment principles, one can imagine mobilising the points of intersection that exist among multiple societies and histories, something the cybernetic revolution and geographic mobility make increasingly possible. Let me offer a single very simple example from the contemporary global stage: struggles over the privatisation of water. Pretty much every time privatisation is proposed, people – whether in Collingwood, Ontario or Cochabamba, Bolivia – defend the idea of water as a common good belonging equally to everyone. The force of this idea in the world right now lies precisely in the fact that, in purely ethnographic terms, it has many genealogies; it has originated on who knows how many different occasions in the course of the history and geography of human groups. In today's global scenario, the idea of water as a common good exists as a point of intersection of multiple genealogies, which have the capacity to resonate with and reinforce each other. Such points present obvious occasions for intercultural agency.

As this example suggests, it is easy now to posit a planetary concept of the human that is superordinate to the 'Indo-European expression'. Recent proposals for the wholesale reworking of knowledge suggest the force of this possibility. Masao Miyoshi, among others, has called for a reorganisation of the pursuit of knowledge under the aegis of ecology and planetary survival. The concept of 'planetarity' is central in the recent epistemic proposals of Gayatri Spivak. Iraqi scholar Ferial Ghazoul insists on a 'subterranean collective self in which we all partake', and a 'promise of global collectivity'.[13] It is no accident that these thinkers all inhabit multiple Western and non-Western intellectual terrains.

The idea of 'the global human' remains heretical to a doctrine many Westerners have installed in their heads: that the human was invented by humanism. But here again we can repeat the point: it is not in the slightest necessary to be occidental or occidentalised in order to conceive of humanity or the human in totalising terms; it can be done from anywhere. Many people felt an imagined planetary *polis* was provisionally brought into being on 15 February 2004, in the unprecedented worldwide demonstration against the invasion of Iraq – not a series of separate demonstrations in different places, but a single demonstration – planetary in scale, archipelagal in form, performative and semantic in character, improvised and imperfect, held together by mobile phones, internet communications, digital images, and imaginations. In this moment of enormous planetary change, marked by polarisation, disposability, disequilibrium and danger, that improvised *polis* was an important Utopian moment.

Even people like myself who, for a long time, saw the term globalisation as a fake alibi for capitalism and empire, now recognise that a new phase in the existence of the planet does seem to be occurring, its outlines still in flux. Three decades of neo-liberal plunder have marked the beginning of something but they are not an endpoint. The disequilibriums they have produced are too great. Over the last decade institutions have begun to multiply at the global or planetary level creating tensions and counterweights against the crushing momentum of the WTO and the IMF: the World Economic Summit in Davos was deliberately counterweighted by the World Social Summit in Porto Alegre. Alongside the World Bank, a World Court is making its appearance. And we've had the set of experiments with world summits – on water in Kyoto; on racism in South Africa. A World Congress of Indigenous Peoples has been meeting every two years for a decade. When Jacques Chirac promised a '*réponse planetaire*' to pandemics like AIDS, he was speaking from a subject position that only relatively recently acquired orthodoxy. Transnational feminism, beginning with the UN Decade for Women, provided many of the templates for these kinds of gatherings. Its immense achievements are often overlooked. Though the hegemony of the rich countries remains in force, these emergent planetary initiatives are symptoms, among many others, of a dynamic multifaceted planetary scenario, quite improvisatory and unpredictable, with new forms of citizenship, agency and politics under construction.

IV

Before I end these remarks, one point may need underscoring. Local tumults and civilisational rhetorics encourage people to think that the very presence of differences naturally or inevitably produces conflict. But this is false. Difference is not inherently a problem. All over the world groups with radically different ways of life and world views (including men and women; old and young) stably coexist, living in all kinds of dynamic arrangements and continually negotiated relationships. The thing we are calling intercultural dialogue goes on all the time without programmatic efforts to construct it. The erroneous and often unconscious notion that difference by nature produces conflict implies, horribly, that homogeneity is somehow some kind of solution. This is entirely false, and also pernicious, insofar as it authorises those in power to suppress differences as a matter of course.

Conflict is not an inevitable by-product of cultural difference, but differences can always erupt into confrontation, or be manipulated into violence. Political interests, competition for power or resources, demands for equality or redress, relocations and demographic alterations – factors such as these mobilise differences into confrontation. It works the other way round too: conflicts generate paradigms of cultural difference with which to give themselves meaning. 'Intercultural dialogue' becomes an object of concern, as in this book, in response to actually existing conflicts. People seek it out as an instrument for resolving or defusing conflicts. Here again, its work is as much performative as semantic. At the level of meaning it seeks mutual knowledge and understanding; at the level of performance it creates occasions for non-violent interchange among conflicting parties.

It also, we should note, takes sides. It is probably important to recognise that the concept of 'intercultural dialogue' emerges from within democratic ideologies that regard inequality and subjugation as undesirable and unjust. From this perspective situations where ideas of difference underwrite the subordination of one group by another appear as in need of intervention. Dialogue becomes an intervention, because it places the unequal parties into a symmetrical exchange. To do this is to take sides with the subordinated party where there is one, to open up conflict between oppressor and oppressed, not defuse it, even as one aims to produce mutual understanding and acceptance.

This ideological grounding in democratic, egalitarian values makes inevitable the familiar points of paradox: how can tolerance include tolerance for intolerance? What can be achieved by a multicultural openness to antidemocratic fundamentalisms? What can intercultural dialogue consist of between parties who value mutual understanding and parties who do not? What kinds of dialogues are actually possible between democratic, egalitarian, anti-essentialist paradigms and hierarchical, fundamentalist, doctrinal paradigms? It's impossible in this brief essay to address these difficult and fascinating questions. Anthropologists and historians will tell you, however, that these are precisely the points at which the most profound learning and growth take place. For one encounters one's own ability to grasp what one finds intolerable. Clifford Geertz makes the point eloquently:

> 'The truth of the doctrine of cultural (or historical – it is the same thing) relativism is that we can never apprehend another people's or another period's imagination neatly, as though it were our own. The falsity of it is that we can therefore never genuinely apprehend it at all. We can apprehend it well enough, at least as well as we apprehend anything else not properly ours; but we do so not by looking *behind* the interfering glosses that connect us to it, but *through* them.'[14]

The encounter with 'powerful sensibilities' radically different from one's own comes, however, 'only at the expense of [one's] inward ease'. 'Whatever use the imaginative productions of other peoples – predecessors, ancestors, or distant cousins – can have for our moral lives,' says Geertz, 'it cannot be to simplify them.' Even as it prizes a certain neutrality, a forceful idea of intercultural dialogue is not then ethically or politically neutral. Even as it seeks to defuse conflict and advance its ideas of justice, it actively seeks out that inward unease and seeks to produce it in others. What makes this necessary and revealing is the fact, to use Geertz's words, that the 'interfering glosses' are both what divide and connect participants in the encounter.

Postscript on language

Vadim Perelman's film *The House of Sand and Fog*, based on the novel by Andre Dubus III, narrates a tragic confrontation between a young Anglo-American woman and an Iranian immigrant who acquires her house by government auction after a miscalculation of her tax liability. At a pivotal point in the story, the distraught woman calls on the Iranian's gentle and unhappy wife to explain the situation. The viewer's hopes rise. Will the women be able to find a just solution where the men are acting by codes of violence and self-interest? The young woman describes what has happened. The wife looks on sympathetically. Then a pause. 'You don't understand a thing I'm saying, do you?' The Iranian wife hands her a paper: 'You write it all down. I show to my husband.' The possibility of a women's solution is blocked by another gendered reality: the sequestered immigrant wife trapped in monolingualism and its attendant dependency. This too is a story with multiple genealogies.

Later, another linguistic failure triggers the film's disastrous climax. The Iranians' teenage son is shot and killed when he attacks a rogue police officer who has been trying to help the young woman recover her house. His reason? The cop has mispronounced his name, calling him Ishmael instead of Esmail. It is the last straw.[15]

The House of Sand and Fog is about immigration, its geopolitics, its transcultural improvisations, its charged, even fatal, poetics. Language and translation are at the heart of these, as they are at the heart of events unfolding as I write in Afghanistan, the Middle East, and Guantánamo.[16] The allusion to *Moby-Dick* is almost too obvious: which is it going to be in 21st-century America? Will Ahab learn to say Esmail, or will Esmail accept a Christianising name change? Language, or rather linguistic difference, determines the tragic plot of Perelman's film, yet its central role is very likely to escape the viewer's notice.

Around the same time that *The House of Sand and Fog* made its debut, the regional leaders of Afghanistan gathered in Kabul to negotiate a constitution. It was a founding moment for a new state.

After weeks, negotiations broke down over a single final point: whether languages of two powerful minority groups, Turkmen and Uzbek, would have official status along with the majority languages, Pashto and Dari. This provision would permit the founding of schools in those languages, for example. The Pashtuns refused to budge. The minority leaders prepared to go home. The UN's Algerian negotiator, Lakhdar Brahimi, shuttled among the sides, and at last a compromise was reached: the minority languages would have official status in the regions where they were spoken. Afghanistan's president, of Dari ethnicity, congratulated the leaders in Uzbek.

It is impossible to think seriously about intercultural dialogue without coming to grips with the linguistic dimensions of today's planetary social, ecological, economic, political and imaginary realignments. It can be hard to see them in part because language is always there; always at work. It is the medium in which both the realigning and the analysis of it are going on. It is also the performance arena. Language is often a revealing symptom of current transformations, but it is also a powerful agent in its own right. Yet its force is almost inevitably overlooked in theorisations of globality, mobility, markets, and geopolitics. In the two anecdotes with which I began this essay, everything depended on the availability of a lingua franca, English, to which participants had uneven access. But, as the Afghanistan negotiations suggest, demands for local linguistic powers can match or trump demands for state languages and transnational lingua francas, and they should. Linguistic heterogeneity is not in itself undesirable, nor is linguistic homogeneity inherently desirable.

The linguistic geography of the planet is changing rapidly, and even the specialists have very little idea what the world will be like linguistically a hundred years from now. For students of intercultural dialogue, that is a formidable challenge.

Endnotes

[1] 'Arts of the Contact Zone', *Profession* (Modern Language Association) 9, 1991: pp. 33–40.

[2] For exploration of this term see Doris Sommer (ed.), Cultural Agency, Durham: Duke University Press, 2004.

[3] In the essay referred to, I defined contact zones as: 'social spaces where cultures meet, clash, and grapple with each other, often in contexts of highly asymmetrical relations of power, such as colonialism, slavery, or their aftermaths'.

[4] I am indebted to performance studies theorist Diana Taylor for my introduction to this term, and related concepts. See Diana Taylor, *The Archive and the Repertoire: Performing Cultural Memory in the Americas,* Durham: Duke University Press, 2003.

[5] See H. Maturana y F. Varela, *Autopoeisis and Cognition: The Realisation of the Living*, London: D. Reidel, 1980, cited in Sylvia Wynter, 'The Ceremony Must Be Found: After Humanism', boundary 2 12:3 and 13:1, special issue on 'Humanism and the University,' spring–fall 1984, 19–70, p. 22.

[6] In the USA, right-wing groups such as the American Council of Trustees and Alumni have appropriated the language of diversity to challenge faculty governance over academic appointments in the name of 'deological diversity'.

[7] Thomas de Zengotita, 'Common Ground: Finding Our Way Back to the Enlightenment', *Harper's magazine*, 306, January 2003: 37.

[8] Paper presented at conference on Critical Cosmopolitanisms, Irvine, California, March 2003.

[9] For further discussion of this concept, see M. L. Pratt, 'Modernity and Periphery: Towards a Global and Relational Analysis', in Elizabeth Mudimbé-Boyi (ed.), *Beyond Dichotomies.* Albany, NY: SUNY UP: pp. 21–47.

[10] Judith Butler, Ernesto Laclau and Slavoj Zizek, *Contingency, Hegemony, Universality: Contemporary Dialogues on the Left*, London and New York: Verso 2000, p. 45. This volume is disappointingly symptomatic of the problem I am diagnosing here. Its discussions of contingency, hegemony and universality take place in entirely Eurocentric terms.

[11] Amartya Sen, 'What's the Point of Democracy?' *Bulletin of the American Academy of Arts and Sciences*, spring 2004, pp. 8–11.

[12] Wynter, 'The Ceremony Must Be Found' (op.cit. note 5), p. 37. Note the performativity of Wynter's call for a ceremony.

[13] I refer to papers presented by these three scholars at the Presidential Forum, Modern Language Association Annual Convention, December 2003. On planetarity see also Gayatri Chakravorty Spivak, *Death of a Discipline*, New York: Columbia University Press, p. 101.

[14] Geertz, Clifford, 'Found in translation: On the social history of the moral imagination', *Local Knowledge: Further essays in interpretive anthropology*. NY: Basic Books, 1983: p. 44.

[15] Both these episodes take place somewhat differently in the novel, which thematises language even more extensively than the film. Dubus studied Farsi for two years to write his novel, and invents a Farsi–English narrative voice that is a linguistic *tour de force*.

[16] Farsi, the language being spoken and misspoken in *The House of Sand and Fog*, has long been on the State Department's list of critical languages.

Building an international organisation

Ron G. Manley OBE

Building any new organisation from scratch is a complex process. Finding the right people, bringing them together, welding them into an efficient and fully functional unit requires patience, perseverance and a lot of luck. Building a new international organisation adds a whole new dimension of complexity to this process. This short essay describes the building of one such organisation: the Technical Secretariat of the Organisation for the Prohibition of Chemical Weapons (OPCW).[1]

The member states of the OPCW decided that its headquarters should be established in The Hague, and in February 1993 a Preparatory Commission was established in that city, along with the first members of a provisional Technical Secretariat to service it. By the time I joined the Secretariat in early September, as Head of its Chemical Demilitarisation Branch, the number of staff had increased to around 20. The Preparatory Commission was to be succeeded by the OPCW when the treaty entered into force, exactly 180 days after 65 countries had ratified it. The 65th country to ratify the Chemical Weapons Convention (CWC) was Hungary, which deposited its ratification document at the United Nations headquarters, in New York, on 31 October 1996. The OPCW and its Technical Secretariat came into being on 27 April 1997.

Finding and recruiting the people

Our Technical Secretariat was to be staffed with between 450 and 500 personnel, drawn exclusively from member states of the OPCW.

The treaty specified that they be appropriately qualified for the task and drawn from as wide a geographical base as possible. Unlike the majority of international Secretariats, whose staff are principally linguists, administrative, legal and secretarial personnel, ours would also include around 270 technically qualified personnel to staff its Inspectorate and Verification Divisions. The requirement was for experienced, professionally qualified, chemical engineers, industrial chemists, chemical weapons specialists, analytical chemists and medical personnel. Finding these people was to prove a lengthy and challenging task, occupying four or five colleagues and myself for much of the next three years.

Initially, the Head of the Secretariat interviewed candidates nominated by the member states and made his selection, taking due note of the need to maintain an appropriate geographical balance – by no means an easy task. While this process worked well during the early days, it was no way to recruit the large number of personnel required at entry into force of the CWC. The proposed 220 inspectors needed to staff the Inspectorate, for example, would have to be recruited in two batches: the first batch of 120 brought on board at entry into force, and the second batch of 80 starting 12 months later.

The problem was how to find these experienced, professionally qualified technical personnel and then persuade them to relocate themselves and their families to the Netherlands, to join an organisation many of them had never heard of, with a starting date – since employment could only commence on a date dependent on the deposit of the 65th ratification – unknown. Staff regulations and rules were still under discussion by the member states. So, we were also unable to guarantee the terms and conditions under which they would be employed.

Nevertheless, information packages – containing a brief description of the organisation and its proposed function, detailed job descriptions for each post, salary scales and provisional terms and conditions of employment – were duly prepared in the six official languages of the United Nations (Arabic, Chinese, English, French, Russian and Spanish) for member states to circulate. Details were placed in English on the organisation's website, which proved one of the more effective ways of attracting potential candidates. The response, despite all these uncertainties, was a steady, if geographically patchy, stream of applications, which was an indication of the level of commitment of the applicants to the objectives of the CWC.

While in general the number of applications from Asia, North America, West and Eastern Europe was satisfactory, the response from many individual countries within these regions was poor, and from Africa and Latin America extremely low. Additional efforts were undertaken to overcome these deficiencies, by placing advertisements in trade journals, or sending a member of the Secretariat staff to talk to relevant national organisations. A Brazilian colleague made a particularly successful trip to Latin America, eliciting another dozen, good, applicants from that region.

Formal meetings of the organisation were conducted in all six official languages using simultaneous translation, but the day-to-day working language of the Secretariat was English. Candidates were, therefore, required to provide an indication of their fluency in English and any other spoken or written languages, as well as their experience for the vacancy for which they were applying. By the end of the process we had received over 1,200 applications from around 70 countries for the 200 inspectors, plus a considerable number for the 70 or so technical posts at HQ.

Drawing up shortlists of candidates for each vacancy or type of vacancy proved to be much more difficult than expected for those of us on each small review panel. Quite apart from the number of factors under consideration – qualifications, relevant experience, language skills, country of origin – there were wide variations in familiarity with completing this type of application form. In answer to the question 'Please give details of your current post', an applicant from Western Europe or North America usually furnished a full description of what the candidate did, often including an extensive CV. Applications from Russia and Eastern Europe might contain a one-line entry, such as 'Head of Analytical Laboratory' for a given company or organisation, or 'Chief Engineer' for a production unit within a company; while those received from Asian candidates often understated the extent of the candidate's actual experience. Since most of the application forms were completed in English, frequently not the applicant's first language, cultural differences and language-related issues were rife. Many times, we were obliged to go back to the applicant or his government for further clarification, before around 400 candidates were finally shortlisted for interview.

We were planning to conduct interviews in English, but it rapidly became clear that this was not going to work. While candidates were often perfectly capable of holding a conversation, understanding highly technical questions and providing equally complex technical answers in English was a different matter. Following one particularly difficult interview with a Chinese candidate in Beijing early on, a member of the panel remarked that the candidate appeared to have a very poor command of the Secretariat's working language. A Chinese colleague politely responded that this was the first opportunity that the candidate had ever had of speaking English with a non-Chinese person, the panel should understand, and that secondly, as the panel was made up of an American, an Australian and a Cornishman, we might like to consider the possible impact of this on the candidate's comprehension. This salutary lesson was fully taken on board. Interviews continued to be held in English, but it became standard practice, wherever practicable, to include a panel member fluent in the candidate's first language.

However, a formal interview with a panel of interviewers is very much a Western concept. For many candidates from Asia and

Eastern Europe, this was a novel experience. Great care was necessary to ensure that candidates were not only put at ease but also provided with an explanation of the interview process and its purpose, so that they did not, albeit inadvertently, undersell themselves.

By this time the recruiting staff had come to the view that, however essential the qualifications and experience for these posts, the key to the creation of a successful international organisation was to recruit staff with the ability to work and function well in a multinational and multicultural environment. One of the more important objectives of the interview, therefore, was to gather sufficient information to enable us to form an opinion on how flexible, and also committed to such an environment candidates were. How well would each cope with living and working together? Were they 'team players'? This is of course very much a subjective measure and not always easy to determine. If asked were they 'team players', those who understood the question would inevitably say 'yes' and those that did not would not know how to answer. Many Asian candidates, for example, are collegiate by nature and culture, and simply did not comprehend the question. A more indirect approach was, therefore, necessary. Candidates, for example, were asked to describe how they dealt with a difficult problem that had occurred during their working career, with superiors, colleagues or subordinates?

Some of us may have had initial prejudices about where this requirement for flexibility and compatibility was most likely to be found. In the event, there was no difficulty in identifying the type in all nationalities and cultures. Having selected our staff, we were now faced with the challenge of establishing them and their families in The Hague.

Getting them on board

The 220 inspectors posed particular problems. While all the

candidates were professionally qualified, there were wide variations in their level and breadth of practical experience. Moreover, few had any detailed knowledge of the CWC or of the role of an on-site inspector. Member states had decided that the two groups would be required to undertake a specially developed, 26-week, training course.

The course was made up of four distinct modules: the first was designed to provide the trainees with a solid understanding of the CWC, the role of the OPCW and the duties, privileges and immunities of its inspectors, as well as a basic grounding in the history and technology of chemical weapons. The second module consisted of a number of specialist courses reinforcing the knowledge of each group of experts. Over a period of about 12 weeks, the analytical chemists, for example, were provided with extensive training in the collection and analysis of samples in the field and the procedures necessary to ensure their integrity and accurate analysis. Chemical engineers and industrial chemists received additional training in chemical industry processes and production methods.

The third module provided training in the actual planning and carrying out of on-site inspections. During this period the trainees, in addition to attending lectures, were formed into teams and given the task of planning a number of inspections. While, by this time, the trainees had been living and working together for a number of months, this was their first opportunity to work together as inspection teams and, at this point, the need for good team skills became paramount. National and cultural differences in the approach to solving problems and getting things done became more evident, and it was necessary for them to learn to overcome this and to appreciate that these differences could be used to their advantage. Intercultural co-operation could be a real boon. Inspections, after all, are an investigative process, and teams made up of people with different backgrounds and approaches to problem solving have a distinct advantage in such situations.

In the final module, inspectors were given the opportunity to plan and carry out inspections at two real facilities located in different member states. Thirteen countries participated in the training programme and the majority of trainees undertook part of their training in at least three or more of these countries.

The majority of the trainees were mid-career professionals. Many of them had held senior positions in their own countries' military or chemical industries. In many cases they were used to having numbers of subordinate staff to support them. A light-hearted comment often heard around the Secretariat was that there were enough Colonels in the Inspectorate to staff several national armies. As inspector trainees, of course, everyone was on an equal footing. They were each expected to join in and undertake their share of the tasks assigned to the team. This was somewhat of a shock for a number of them and some found it easier to adapt to their new situation than others.

But inspection is very much a team game. Once an inspection team leaves The Hague *en route* to the inspection site, it is basically on its own. They will of course receive support from the host country, but the success of the inspection all comes down in the end to each member of the team not only carrying out his or her assigned tasks, but co-operating fully with the others. An important purpose of the training, of course, was to enhance these team skills. But something much more subtle was working itself out during the six months in which the same trainees learned to depend on each other for support and companionship, both during work and leisure time. A lot of assumptions were challenged and expectations reversed. Those who trained in Russia, for example, found that when off duty they were almost entirely dependent on their Russian-speaking colleagues to get around and enjoy the local food. Even when they were in countries where they spoke the language, or English was understood, those familiar with the local culture were able to help those who were not. This was the beginning of a different kind of interdependence and mutual respect: something closer to a celebration of difference, an ingenuity, which over and over again would stand the new inspectors in good stead.

The course provided them with the opportunity to travel, live and work, for an extended period, with other trainees coming from different backgrounds and with differing levels of experience. When you walked into the coffee bar or canteen, people were not grouped by nationality or culture but by the bonds of friendship. The sight of a table with people of six or seven nationalities sitting around it would not even warrant a second glance. Quite simply, the understandings formed during this period enabled the inspectors to function as a tight-knit and effective group. This proved to be the most valuable element of the whole training programme. It brought considerable, long-term, benefits to the Technical Secretariat and its staff.

Over two periods, a month at a time, inspectors successfully completing their course travelled with their families from around 65 countries to arrive in The Hague. Absorbing so many people in such a short space of time requires a lot of patience on all sides. An extensive familiarisation programme was put together, under which local estate agents briefed them on the city, types of property available and typical rental costs or purchase prices. New arrivals were bussed around the city to see the different residential locations. Banks provided briefings on the Dutch banking system, while representatives from International, English and French schools vied for the opportunity to educate their children. Briefings were available on Dutch laws, the medical system and culture. Major Dutch institutions, such as banks and insurance companies, generously offered documentation in English. Somehow, the 'great influx' was accomplished without too much mishap.

Establishing communication

English was the only language of which all 68 nationalities had some knowledge. The staff's command of English varied considerably, however, and establishing a common degree of understanding was by no means an easy task. My own deputy from Belarus spoke very little English when he first arrived. As I could not speak Russian, this led to many interesting exchanges during our first months of working together. Fortunately, we had a young American intern in the Branch who just happened to speak Russian, and was perfectly willing to help out when we got really stuck. Subsequently our two families became firm friends: we often think back on those early days with amusement.

The situation was further complicated by the fact that, with the exception of some of the South Africans, virtually none of the international staff or their families spoke Dutch. Fortunately the Dutch are very tolerant about language and English is widely understood throughout the Netherlands. It fell to the locally recruited staff of the Technical Secretariat to help sort out problems for the families of internationally recruited staff, many of whom spoke neither Dutch nor English, as they wrestled with local authorities and other institutions. Embassies based in The Hague also played a valuable part in assisting their nationals to establish themselves in the city.

Of course, communication problems were not confined to a lack of a vocabulary, but also reflected the widely different national and cultural backgrounds. During the early days this led to considerable confusion. A sense of humour and much patience were vital commodities.

Native English speakers had to learn to adapt their vocabulary, phrasing and use of language. It was soon obvious that those for whom English was a second language often had a better understanding of English grammar than they did. Moreover, participants frequently found their lectures among the most difficult, thanks in part to the number of colloquialisms they unwittingly employed. When an English member of staff accused his Japanese colleague of 'pulling his leg', a lengthy and detailed explanation ensued.

Right from its inception the Technical Secretariat bought into the concept of an electronic office. All documents were produced, edited, circulated and stored within the organisation electronically. Every member of staff, therefore, was expected to be computer literate and capable of typing their own documents and letters. This, in itself, was a considerable shock to many, used to relying on secretaries in their previous posts. The level of IT experience among the new staff varied from highly competent to zero, and a major education programme was necessary to bring everybody up to an acceptable level.

While the member states were responsible for establishing policy, the development of the associated administrative and operational procedures was the responsibility of the Secretariat. In fact, completing this work for the new organisation was a major task. With such a mixture of nationalities and backgrounds, everyone of course had their own solution to any given problem, and the secret was to try and find a common approach. The most successful way of doing this was to get the interested parties around a table and keep them there until agreement was reached. As working relationships became established, this task became noticeably easier.

Creating a common ethos

One of the principal indicators of a successful organisation is the presence of a common ethos or organisational culture; a set of standards of behaviour and performance accepted by all. Such an organisational culture does not automatically appear when a new organisation is created. It has to be actively encouraged.

In a new international, multicultural, organisation there is the added complication of deciding whose cultural standards should form the basis of what is or is not acceptable behaviour. In reality the only way this can be achieved is for the organisation, along with the full co-operation of its staff, to create its own, individual, culture. This requires both patience and time and, despite its importance, will normally have to be undertaken in parallel with its normal activities.

The Technical Secretariat was no exception. Its establishment could not proceed in a vacuum. During its formative period, it had to interact with the outside world and, in particular, with the member states of the OPCW. The day-to-day role of providing assistance and support to the member states had to continue to be met and the Secretariat's verification role including on-site inspections, began in earnest approximately one month after entry into force of the CWC. At that time its new headquarters was still under construction and the staff were temporarily located at three different sites across The Hague. During this period the priority for both Senior Management and the staff of the Technical Secretariat was simply to survive to the end of each day.

Over the following months, however, order gradually took over from chaos and it was possible to begin looking at what we had created. With hindsight, the chaos of those early months actually made a significant contribution to the formation of the Secretariat's culture. The sheer volume of work that had to be completed forced staff rapidly to establish working relationships and to trust and depend upon each other. People simply had to be prepared to compromise. Gradually, many came to realise that the breadth of experience available in working with people from different cultures and backgrounds was a distinct advantage. There was no shortage of new ideas and different approaches to solving the many problems that arose.

There were, of course, numerous disagreements and misunderstandings *en route*. But the overriding desire to get on top of the task meant that these had to be either swiftly resolved or put aside. This is one area where the members of the inspectorate had a distinct advantage over the rest of the Secretariat staff. The six months they had spent living and working together during their training course had provided them with a great opportunity to sort out differences and establish effective working relationships. Headquarters staff, on the other hand, were expected to arrive, find themselves somewhere to live, and start work. For some of them, a rather longer period of adjustment proved necessary.

As time passed, working relationships and behaviour patterns gradually began to evolve which were acceptable to the majority of the staff. One example of this was the use of e-mail. As everyone had access to a networked terminal one of the primary means of communication within the Secretariat was e-mail. The problem is that people will often write things in an e-mail or adopt a manner or tone that they would not use in a face-to-face conversation. While in some cultures this may not cause too many difficulties, in a multicultural organisation it can lead to serious misunderstanding. It was, therefore, necessary to alert staff to this problem and constantly remind them of the importance of avoiding the pitfalls associated with badly or inappropriately worded e-mails.

Building on the emphasis they had put on multicultural flexibility since the early recruiting days, senior management decided to assist the process by bringing in a team of international consultants to provide training for staff at all levels in good management practices and working relationships. A change management team, headed by the Deputy Director-General and with team members representing staff at all levels, was established, given the task of consulting the staff, and drawing up recommendations for ways to improve the Secretariat's operation and culture. This process established an effective two-way communication process between the senior management and the staff. Management became better informed of the issues that were of concern for the staff and staff came to appreciate some of the constraints under which the management had to operate. Over time the Technical Secretariat has developed its own ethos and culture. While it is far from perfect it nevertheless does provide a core set of values against which the behaviour of individuals within the organisation can be judged. Tolerance with respect to cultural and religious differences, equal treatment of men and women and the need to treat other staff members with courtesy are all part of these core values.

One of the spontaneous developments was for the various national or cultural groups to organise a party on their important national or religious days, to which all staff and their families were invited. As a result we celebrated the Chinese New Year, Independence Day, Eid al-Fitr – the feast at the end of Ramadan, and Diwali – the Hindu festival of lights. This did a great deal to enhance our understanding of each other's cultures and beliefs.

Trials and tribulations

But it would be naïve to assume that all of the teething problems in setting up such an organisation can be speedily resolved. Membership of the OPCW was also growing throughout this period, increasing from 87 countries at entry into force to 164 countries today. Whenever possible the OPCW operates by consensus. The decision-making process, therefore, can be both complex and prolonged. While such delays are inevitable in any organisation with as large a number of interested parties as this nevertheless it has, on occasion, made the task of the Technical Secretariat more difficult than it needed to be.

Perhaps the best example of this is the age-old problem of funding. In the case of the OPCW and its Technical Secretariat, the operating costs are met by the member states. Each member state, therefore, has a keen interest in the organisation's programme of work and the budget necessary to support it. Add to this the fact that there were no historical cost data in the early years, against which a proposed budget for the agreed programme of work could be validated, and you have a recipe for disagreement. The outcome is that the member states have had considerable difficulty each year in reaching consensus on these items. During the first five years of its life, in common with so many international organisations, the

Technical Secretariat suffered from chronic under-funding, which inevitably took its toll on staff morale.

Another major staff issue was the question of tenure. At a very early stage in the life of the organisation, the member states expressed the view that the Technical Secretariat should not be a career organisation. Total service within the Secretariat would be limited to a maximum number of years. Before entry into the CWC, however, no decision had been reached on how many years, or how the policy would be implemented. A final decision on this issue was only reached in 2003, six years after the Technical Secretariat came into being. As a result, a high proportion of current staff will be required to leave over the next three years. Again, the delay in reaching consensus wreaks its own havoc on staff morale, and will probably continue to do so over the next few years.

Benefits and rewards

Irrespective of such differences, the staff of the Technical Secretariat and the representatives of the member states are all striving for a common goal, the global elimination of chemical weapons. The overriding commitment of the staff to the purpose of the OPCW and their understanding of the need to get on with the task helped to generate a common spirit and a willingness to compromise. This was what brought them into the organisation, and it was a major factor in their willingness to accept the inevitable difficulties.

But did we think it would work from the outset? Did we heck! We saw the need, but also the huge obstacles. No one could have expected the amazing energy and dedication that was generated by this group of 'people from everywhere'.

In my experience the benefits of working in and helping to create such a new international organisation, far outweigh the disadvantages. Whatever the frustrations, the opportunity to work and live in such a multicultural and multinational environment, provides immeasurable benefits. Gaining an understanding of other cultures and learning to see things from their point of view is just one of these. The opportunity to enjoy the friendship of people from many different countries and backgrounds is another. The realisation that, irrespective of background and culture, the majority of people in the world are seeking the same things, that is, the opportunity to live and raise their children in a moderately comfortable and peaceful environment, is the subtlest of all gentle bonds.

During my time with the OPCW I was fortunate enough to travel to many parts of the world, making friends in many countries. I look back on the eight years I spent living and working in this environment with great affection. I would not have missed one day of it.

Endnotes

[1] The OPCW oversees the implementation of *The Convention on the Prohibition of the Development, Production, Stockpiling and Use of Chemical Weapons and on their Destruction* to give it its full title, or the CWC as it is more conveniently known. At the time of writing, 162 countries have either ratified or acceded to the CWC. Finally opening for signature in Paris in January 1993 after almost 20 years of negotiation, the CWC required its member states to forgo the development, production, stockpiling and use of chemical weapons and to destroy any that they possess within a set timeframe. All facilities used for the production of chemical weapons must either be destroyed or converted for use for peaceful purposes. Member states of the CWC are also required to declare and submit to inspection by OPCW inspectors, chemical production facilities, whether commercial or military, that produce certain, specified, toxic chemicals or the precursor chemicals necessary for their synthesis.

Intercultural dialogue in a multilingual world

Susan Bassnett

In May 2004, President Bush apologised to the world for the treatment of Iraqi prisoners-of-war by US servicemen. Sitting in a hotel room, tuned in to CNN, I listened to an interview with the London Ambassador of the Arab League. The conversation hinged on the issue of what the President had said. He had not apologised, the Ambassador declared, expressing his concern and noting that, 'he only said he was sorry'. The interviewer suggested that thismight be hair-splitting: surely saying sorry is the same as apologising? The ambassador insisted that it was not. The President had failed to apologise.

I reflected at length on this exchange. Which sentence in English appears more persuasive: 'I apologise wholeheartedly' or 'I am very sorry'? Can we distinguish between the sincerity of these two statements? My first reaction was to feel that saying sorry appeared more heartfelt than a formal apology because it implies that some personal process of contrition has been involved. To apologise is the more formal, hence more distant register. Saying sorry seems to carry more personal weight.

But the instant one moves out of English, the distinction is less clear. Were I to apologise formally in Italian, I might use a phrase requesting the offended party to pardon me, such as '*Chiedo scusa*'. This formulation makes me the appellant. I ask for my apology to be accepted, and the communication loop is not closed until my request is granted. After all, apology is a dual process, involving more than one person in the interaction. That dimension is missing in

English. Ironically, the very insistence on the personal carried by the idea of saying one is sorry focuses attention wholly on the speaker, not on anyone else.

President Bush, making his apology, had said he was sorry. In the English-speaking world, this phrase might be read as more sincere, more honest, than the formal verb to apologise. But given that the notion of apology in so many languages involves a two-stage process, first of asking and then of being granted pardon, it is easy to see how a seemingly innocent linguistic usage in one language can be interpreted totally differently in another. Perhaps his advisers should have told him that. By saying he was sorry rather than by asking to be forgiven, he was creating an impression of arrogant self-sufficiency for speakers used to a linguistic system other than English. How often do we all do things that are sincerely meant, couched in the terms that we understand and believe to be appropriate, only to be completely misunderstood by the very people to whom we most want to reach out?

Language and culture can never be separated. Language has been described as the heart in the body of culture, a metaphor aptly illustrating their interconnectedness. The linguistic relativist school of thought, pioneered by Edward Sapir and Benjamin Lee Whorf, argues that different languages reveal different ways of conceptualising the world, and that no two languages can ever be sufficiently similar to reflect the same social reality. Languages are different and the realities that are expressed in language are also different. Anyone with knowledge of more than one language quickly learns that what can be said in one language may be inexpressible in another. Bilinguals negotiate such differences, making adjustments that come close at times to personality shifts.

But cultural relativism is an uncomfortable proposition, because it runs so counter to what so many politicians would have us believe, i.e. that it is entirely possible to communicate perfectly across languages and cultures because contemporary human beings share universal aims. Linguistic difference can easily be bridged, they argue: all we need are trained translators and interpreters to guide us across the frontiers of language. What is said in one language can and must be translatable into another. No matter if we do not know any other languages: provided we have someone to interpret for us, all will be well.

Such a view is hopelessly naïve. Translators and interpreters do, of course, play a vital role in international communication, but they are not all-powerful. The reality is that it is extremely difficult first to acknowledge that difference exists, and then, once difference is recognised, to begin the enormous task of negotiating the cultural divide. An illusion of sameness provides comfort and makes for an easier, quieter life for those who choose to remain blinded to the responsibility they must take when communicating with others in today' s world. But it remains an illusion.

Writing in *The Sunday Times* on 23 May 2004, Amir Taheri, an Iranian Muslim writer, argues that it is impossible to understand a civilisation without knowledge of the language that shapes it. He posits this before moving on to his principal argument, which is that democracy as a concept is incompatible with Islam, since democracy as a system comes from a completely different historical tradition. Taheri points out that the word only started to enter Muslim languages in the late 19th century. The terminology used in political discourse, even the notion of politics itself, is radically different in Islam from other cultures. His reasoning is thought-provoking: Islam is about certainty (*iqan*) while democracy is about doubt. Islam cannot allow people to do as they please, even 'in the privacy of their bedrooms', because God is always 'present, all-hearing and all-seeing'. There is consultation in Islam (*wa shawerhum fil amr*). But, here, consultation is about 'specifics only', never about the overall design of society. In democracy there is a constitution that can be amended or changed. The Qur'an, however, is the immutable word of 'God, beyond amendment or change'.

Taheri, as a Muslim, is not seeking in any way to criticise Islam for this; rather he criticises those in the West who take what he condemns as a fashionable, postmodernist, multicultural stance that refuses to recognise the extent of cultural differences. Islam, he suggests, needs to be engaged in dialogue with other cultures, and it needs to be subjected to critical scrutiny for its own benefit and the benefit of the world in the future. At the same time, the West should beware of making assumptions about universality that are simply untenable. There are great differences between Islamic and Christian cultures – differences of history, culture and belief – and these are articulated through language.

The fashionable approach that disquiets Taheri has its origins in good intentions. It has evolved from well-meaning liberal humanist sentiments in Britain and the United States, and stands in stark and necessary contrast to the discourse of those who attack Islam as 'barbaric' or 'medieval' or 'primitive', using a language that implies that Western cultures are further up the evolutionary scale than others. This attitude derives from the superficial, but widespread, Western faith in the virtues of modernity and ever-increasing progress, a social model that sees dynamic change as more desirable than maintenance of a status quo. The problem here is that technological progress (for example, improvements in health care, transport or communication systems) is equated with social progress, so that modernity is represented as bringing with it a more desirable set of attitudes and behaviours. Those societies that give greater weight to traditional behaviour patterns are dismissed as out-of-date and out of touch with the modern world and progress.

This point can be illustrated by the heated debate that has gone on for decades now in the West about whether the veil is an instrument of female oppression or not. European and American feminist activists flew to Iran in 1979, after the Revolution, to express their solidarity with sisters 'forced' to wear the veil, only to discover that many women had chosen to do so deliberately. In 2002, Cherie

Blair and Laura Bush pledged to free Afghan women from the veil. In 2003 the French government banned the use of headscarves among Muslim schoolgirls. The veil was, in each of these cases, interpreted from a non-Muslim perspective, and thereby condemned as part of a primitive culture. Women covered their heads in Christian Europe for centuries; but the demise of head-covering in Europe has been interpreted through the deceptive lens of continuous modernisation. The relationship between public and private behaviour that is and always will be differently seen and differently negotiated in different cultures is no longer respected when it comes to some Western attitudes to the veil. From an Islamic viewpoint, the veil is both symbolic and functional, serving both as a sign of femininity and as a means of preventing women from being exposed to brutal language and behaviour. But as the West looks at the *burqa* in horror, meanwhile other cultures look at English football supporters with revulsion and ponder what social and family values such people reflect. If the veiling of women is regarded in some places as a sign of a less advanced culture, so football hooliganism is regarded by others as a sign of the moral decadence of a society that has lost its faith and its ideals.

Hitting the reef

In September 2002, the British Council invited me to represent the UK at an event organised by the Mayor of Rome, which brought together on one platform intellectuals from several European countries a year after 9/11. The title of the event was provocative: *Un dialogo naufragato*?, which translates literally into 'A shipwrecked dialogue?' or, in standard English, 'Has (intercultural) dialogue hit a reef?' Underpinning the question was the apocalyptic notion that global dialogue had indeed foundered irrevocably, that the events of September 11 had changed the world's consciousness, and that despite the millions of words that circulate round the globe every day, despite the communications revolution that has given us internet cafés in rainforests and oases, despite the perpetually 'breaking news' on television channels 24 hours a day, 365 days a year, we are less able to talk to one another than at any point in history and certainly less able to listen and try to understand what others are saying to us.

What makes this doubly ironic is that the last decades of the 20th century saw the spread of global English eclipsing every other language on the planet. English has become the language of international business, of diplomacy, of mass communication. Millions of people on every continent use English either as a primary or secondary language. Surely one might presume that this will have facilitated communication, placing the idea of international dialogue more in our reach. Yet if English has proved to be a useful instrument in many ways, another aspect to the global English phenomenon has received scant attention. Within the English-speaking world of Britain, the United States and Australasia, interest in learning other languages, never particularly strong, has gone into sharp decline, with the consequence that those nations find themselves more isolated from the rest of the world and less able to recognise, let alone appreciate, cultural differences. Indeed, it could be argued that for all those countries, the English language has become an export commodity, and that linguistic colonialism has replaced the 19th century variety. That knowledge of English should be seen as so desirable only compounds the problem; why learn another language when everyone else is learning yours?

The objective of learning another language has always been to communicate with others. At times that communication has been through literacy, through reading works written in other languages and consequently being able to access the culture and history of others. More recently, the objective has been primarily verbal. Learning a language has been seen as a means of enabling people to talk to one another. Once linguistic competence is established, it is assumed that acquaintance with the history and culture of others will follow. But the rise of global English and the decline of foreign language learning means that international communication patterns are changing. Those who have learned English in addition to their own language or languages are able to acquire an understanding of the difficulties of communicating across cultures that is not possible for monolingual speakers. Knowing only one language in today's world reduces our ability to become acquainted with other ways of thinking and behaving. More people speaking English does nothing to alter this state of affairs.

The early 18th and 19th century European Orientalist scholars were passionately committed to learning the ancient and modern languages of Asia, in order to have some greater understanding of the broader cultural context. Paradoxically, colonialism inspired some invaluable scholarship, for alongside the history of exploitation that is now well recognised, there was another history, that deriving from a genuine desire to learn more about other cultures. Today, as that learning has fallen into disuse, the United Kingdom and the United States will have to recruit a new generation to learn the languages of those cultures that they particularly need to understand better. For being able to comprehend alternative perspectives is essential for any dialogue. The point that Taheri is making in comparing the relationship between individual human beings and the state, goes well beyond linguistic difference: he argues that Islam and the West have for centuries not only evolved different systems of government, based on totally different principles, but that these differences are enshrined in language and consequently in perception. Exporting English to the world carries with it an assumption that values articulated in English can also be exported, understood and accepted.

Yet this is plainly not the case. Despite the endless rhetoric in the Western media about the importance of establishing a genuinely democratic government in Afghanistan, with full representation of all social groups, this has not happened. Any historian would have known that it could not happen. Gender, tribal and ethnic politics in Afghanistan are complex in ways that the West cannot comprehend. What needs to be borne in mind is that societies evolve differently, and that although there may be a basis for understanding, the values of one cannot and should not be imposed upon another.

The current schism within the worldwide Anglican Church is a good example of what happens when one set of cultural assumptions, in this case the presumption that homosexuality must be universally acceptable, is rejected by other cultures. That the American, Canadian and English churches wish to put an end to discrimination against homosexuals is entirely appropriate to many people within those contexts, but totally unacceptable in many African and Asian cultures. This debate is interesting because what is at stake is no doctrinal matter, but a cultural issue. What it reveals, as clearly as the debates about veiling show, is that cultural differences need to be acknowledged, not ignored or overruled and certainly not dismissed as somehow more antiquated or even more 'primitive'. For the underlying assumption of such terminology is that the dissenting social groups will eventually catch up with the more forward-thinking modern world represented by the dominant cultures, if only given time. Uncomfortable though this may be to admit to, this position can only be described as a form of cultural imperialism.

The West has placed increasing emphasis on modernity, even going so far as to equate modernity with freedom. Yet this emphasis on modernity is not without its own problems. For a start, it can lead to the loss of knowledge. In the UK, the urge to promote the new at the expense of the old has all kinds of ramifications. Many people deplore the practice in most British public libraries of disposing of books that look old-fashioned or which have not been taken out as frequently as others, leaving shelves stacked only with contemporary best-sellers. This practice mirrors broader social patterns: British politicians, advertisers and retailers sell their products by claiming to offer benefits for the future through improvements over the past. The adjectives 'new', 'improved', 'better' and 'better than ever' are strewn through magazines, advertisements, consultation papers and government documents in equal measure. But the obsession with modernity is by no means universal. Other cultures value traditional practices, and view the present through eyes that are trained also on the past, seeking continuity.

Knowledge of more than one language soon exposes the fallacy of universal claims. Of course the human body suffers pain, hunger, joy and grief everywhere in the world, but how those emotions manifest themselves, how they are internalised and then narrated is not universal. In the West, we have a binary ethical code that divides good from evil; other cultures have systems that organise their ethics differently. Some languages have terms for complex kinship systems, and can distinguish cousins on the mother's side several stages removed; while English resorts to the phrase 'in-law' and does not even have words to differentiate maternal and paternal blood relatives. Some languages have sophisticated abstract terms for states of mind, while others do not.

Different languages have different colour spectrums, different concepts of tense, even different ways of visualising past, present and future. We see the future as before us, the past behind. Others, following the logic of the body, see the future as behind, where the eyes cannot see, and the past before them since it has already happened and therefore can still be seen. With so many linguistic differences, we ought to live in a state of heightened awareness in this age of mass communication. Instead, CNN embodies a communication gap, yawning over an apology born in one context, but unacceptable to another.

Bridging the gap

In my contribution to the Rome seminar, I argued that the gap that certainly exists between cultures need not be seen as wholly negative, for it serves to remind us of the importance of difference in our multifaceted world. We need to negotiate difference, but in order to begin the process of negotiation we first have to recognise that differences exist and learn to value them. Homogenising, whether through the lingua franca that some claim English has become, or through the transmission of the same image in global news bulletins on television channels across the world, does not help communication. Yet until recently there has been an anxiety about highlighting difference, perhaps because of the residual belief that once differences are established, they will be instantly hierarchised, with someone always in a superior position.

In his novel, *Things Fall Apart*, Chinua Achebe draws a picture that consciously fills in the gaps left by Joseph Conrad in his portrayal of Africa in *Heart of Darkness*. Through the narration of his protagonist Marlow, Conrad paints a frightening portrait of the dark impulses that underpin colonialism. The novel is written from a European perspective; the African inhabitants are mysterious, shadow-like, sinister. Achebe's novel starts from the opposite point of view, from that of the African village community into which white people come. In this novel, the strange, mysterious, sinister figures are the Europeans, as the fabric of the old society starts to break down under pressure from external influences.

Recently, I read a number of students' essays comparing these novels, and was impressed by the sensitivity and sophistication that young people could bring to their reading. What they could see clearly were the conflicting moral positions of both writers, and by looking at these two very differently written works, they were able to negotiate layers of signification and find ways of relating that negotiation to their own time. Both Conrad and Achebe, in different ways and at different times, recognised the need for a broader, more pluralistic perspective; and today's students, by setting these novels side by side, are learning about difference and about negotiation. They are also learning about history, in this case the history of colonialism, and the need to continue to keep the past under negotiation.

Societies that focus too much on modernity run the risk of forgetting their own past. Ironically in an age when more people than ever before are literate, cultural amnesia is a growing phenomenon. Sometimes temporary amnesia is an important part of regeneration: China needs to move on beyond the horrors of the cultural revolution, while other states need to move on beyond civil wars, totalitarian regimes, military occupation or genocide. To dwell on horrors that have occurred at the expense of building the new is counterproductive. Cultural amnesia, or selective remembering, enables societies to rethink themselves, to airbrush out difficult decades or even centuries, and to represent themselves anew to the world. But it is also important, when the time is right, for the past to be reinstated in some way, reassessed and re-examined, so that the present makes more sense, and lessons are applied as people move into the future.

Britain, Australia and the United States have some uncomfortable history to confront. It is hard to come to terms with the story of slavery and the racial apartheid that continued in the United States for so long; the abomination and brutality of the West Indian plantations; the history of the British in India; the carving up of Africa without regard for tribal homelands; the treatment of aboriginal peoples and countless other examples of discrimination and prejudice. Apologies have been made publicly, though given our earlier discussion of the two-stage process involved, the value of such gestures is questionable.

A better way to apologise to the dead is to listen to the living, endeavouring to understand the historical processes and contexts that led to the events we now struggle to comprehend and atone for. Admittedly, history is strangely taught today, particularly in Britain, where it is not even part of the national curriculum in schools. But perhaps as a reaction against this marginalisation, we are currently witnessing a huge popular upsurge of interest in history, in publishing, film and television. I see this as a hopeful sign, as an indication of the strength of grass-roots impulses as people strive to understand more about themselves and about others. For history is intimately connected to identity, and identity is in turn intimately connected to language.

Back to religious faith

Taheri complains about what he describes as the 'everything-is-equal-to-everything-else fashion of postmodernist multiculturalism and political correctness'. Such thinking, he suggests, prevents us from acknowledging differences and acknowledging that there might be some differences that are irreconcilable.

For genuine dialogue between civilisations to happen, there must be clarity on all sides, and that clarity is as much about knowing who we are as about knowing who the other is. To know who we are means understanding from whence we have come. Understanding more about ourselves is a good starting point from which to begin learning about others and to negotiate differences that may be unbridgeable.

Wherever we find irreconcilable difference, precisely there we may find the beginnings of a new understanding. Take the difference prominent in our world today, over the value or otherwise of martyrdom. Although Christianity still venerates the early Christian martyrs prepared to die for their beliefs centuries ago, today those men and women who opt for martyrdom, be they Islamic or Sikh or Christian fundamentalist remain outside Western comprehension. Every so often, someone advances the hypothesis that those seeking martyrdom come from deprived backgrounds and that more poverty relief will solve the problem. Others offer pragmatic solutions: solve x or y political situation such as Palestine or Chechnya, and the desirability of martyrdom will fade away.

Such arguments are typically European in that they are based on reason. The rational approach invites us to look at the broader picture and seek an explanation that has a clear social cause. But what remains missing is the cultural significance of martyrdom in some specific geographical and ideological contexts. The men who flew the planes on 9/11 were not from deprived homes; nor were they driven by any single specific political cause. Suicide bombers in South-East Asia do not act as they do because the Russians have not found a satisfactory solution to unrest in Chechnya.

The West, with its belief in reason and its desire for continuous progress is failing at the present time to deal with the importance of religious faith – still an immensely powerful force in the lives of millions. Part of the process of thinking about why death should present any kind of option for many well-educated young people in today's world, will involve looking at why so many people, particularly in Britain, are so uncomfortable with religion. The fact that both the British Prime Minister and the US President are church-going Christians is often the subject of satire and derision, rather than a cause for celebration. Yet, at the same time, both left and right deplore what they see as the collapse of community and family values in society in general. Is this not a great contradiction that deserves exploring?

I am not suggesting that the way forward is for the mass reinstatement of formalised religion, nor that the study of history will necessarily improve international understanding. What I am suggesting is that in order for us to move the dialogue forward, we need to understand more about our own societies, about where we have come from and why such great changes have taken place in such a short time, and we need also to be more aware of the difference between how we see the world and how others see it. Simply assuming that we are communicating perfectly because other people speak a version of English is dangerous, because it is premised on an assumption of sameness between cultures that is patently false. Knowledge of different languages is a first step, because then we can begin to grasp the immense differences between cultures, and start to explore ways of building bridges.

'Intercultural awareness training'

It is ridiculously Utopian to suppose that by reintroducing foreign language study in schools we shall transform our world. What we can do, however, is to promote the message of cultural difference in a positive manner, abandoning the misleading idea that all cultures are fundamentally the same, but not falling into the trap of claiming the superiority of one cultural system over another.

We need to train future generations to become more aware of difference, to take pride in their own identity while reaching out to others without prejudice or implicit belief in their own superiority. What is termed in the jargon 'intercultural awareness training' should be an intrinsic part of education at all levels, and this should mean much more than simply recognising the need for different politeness strategies in different contexts or learning how to ask for a cup of coffee in another language. It should entail exploring differences in conceptualising the world between different cultures – considering such questions as how different peoples view the significance of individuality versus the authority of the family; the role of the state in private life; the importance of religious faith and the presence of God in daily life; the meaning of history in the shaping of identity; and the importance of place and the values attached to life and to death.

The easiest place to start may be through an exploration of the differences between languages. Once we can all understand why President Bush's apology was so badly received in many parts of the world, why saying sorry was not felt to be adequate because it was seen to be a statement of arrogance rather than of humility, we can start to engage in a type of dialogue that has less likelihood of being shipwrecked during the voyage.

Contributors

Mary Louise Pratt is Silver Professor of Spanish and Portuguese Language and Literature at New York University, and a graduate of the University of Toronto and Stanford University. She is author of *Toward a Speech Act Theory of Literary Discourse* (1978) and *Imperial Eyes* (1992), and co-author of *Linguistics for Students of Literature* (1980) and *Women, Culture and Politics in Latin America* (1990). Her current work concerns the social imaginaries of neo-liberalism and the emergence of planetary thought. She is also writing on language policy in relation to global mobilities and the changing faces of multilingualism. Formerly Olive H. Palmer Professor of Humanities at Stanford University, she participated for many years in debates there about US multiculturalism.

Ron G. Manley, OBE was awarded a BA, with first-class honours, in Chemistry and Materials Science and joined the UK Ministry of Defence in 1960, where he worked for more than 30 years in a range of fields related to the development of effective defensive measures against the use of chemical weapons. He is a Chartered Chemist, Member of the Royal Society of Chemistry and a Chartered Member of the Institute of Occupational Safety and Health. He joined the Organisation for the Prohibition of Chemical Weapons (OPCW) in 1993 and served with the Organisation until his retirement at the end of 2001. During that time, he held the posts of Head of the Chemical Demilitarisation Branch (1993–97), Special Adviser to the Director-General of the OPCW (1997–2000), and Director of the Verification Division (2000–01). He is currently a freelance consultant on arms control and chemical and biological warfare issues.

Susan Bassnett is Professor in the Centre for Translation and Comparative Cultural Studies at the University of Warwick. She is a world expert in the field of translation and intercultural studies, author of the international best-seller *Translation Studies*, and has also published extensively in comparative literature, theatre studies and modern languages. She is well-known for her journalism and media work, and is currently director of a three-year Arts and Humanities Research Board-funded project on 'The Cultural Politics and Economics of Language and Translation in Global Media'. She takes a keen interest in regional and national policy for the arts, and chairs the board of the Warwick Arts Centre. She has four children and a baby grandson and lives in North Warwickshire with numerous animals.

Nick Wadham-Smith is Deputy Director of Counterpoint, the British Council's cultural relations think tank in London. In the 1970s he studied with the cultural theorist Terry Eagleton, and has a long-standing interest in the relationship between culture and society. Later, teaching English in President Sadat's Egypt provided a valuable insight into intercultural education. At the British Council he founded and edited the organisation's international magazine focusing on comparative cultural studies of the UK, *British Studies Now* (1992–2003), and, in 2004, its successor, *Thresholds*, a publication for professionals working across cultures. Conferences for the British Council include *Re-inventing Britain*, 1997, (developed with Homi K. Bhabha) and *Looking into England*, 1999, (with Susan Bassnett), the seminar series, *Representing Cultures, and Connecting Flights, new cultures of the diaspora*, a collaboration with Arts Council England. He is director of *Eye to Eye*, the first global cultural relations conference, to be held in London in November 2004, and co-author, with Martin Rose, of *Mutuality, Trust & Cultural Relations* (2004).